SAMSON

Judges 13–16 for Children
Written by Loyal Kolbrek and Chris Larson
Illustrated by Glenn Myers

ARCH® Books
Copyright © 1970, 1994 Concordia Publishing House
3558 S. Jefferson Avenue, St. Louis, MO 63118-3968
Manufactured in the United States of America

Samson had a secret.
He knew he was to be
A Nazirite—God's servant
To set his people free.

He traveled down to Timnah,
And near a vineyard there,
A lion strong attacked him.
Its roaring filled the air.

God's Spirit came to Samson—
No weapon could be found.
He tore apart the lion
And threw it on the ground.

Philistine men caught Samson
With new ropes, tightly bound.
God's Spirit came upon him;
The ropes fell to the ground.

The jawbone of a donkey
Was found nearby, and then,
With this his only weapon,
He killed a thousand men!

Then his enemies waited
At Gaza, by the gate.
They planned to capture Samson;
Their hearts were filled with hate.

But Samson left at midnight.
He left without a sound.
And as he passed the gateposts,
He tore them from the ground.

He put them on his shoulders
And took them miles away.
He left them on a hilltop
Before the light of day.

Samson loved a woman.
Delilah was her name;
And to her home one evening,
Philistine rulers came.

When Samson came to see her,
She said, "Please tell me true,
How you can kill your enemies,
Without them hurting you?"

"If they use rope," he told her,
"A new rope it must be.
If they bind my hands up tightly,
I cannot break them free."

She bound him; then she shouted,
"Philistine men are here!"
He snapped the ropes off quickly.
The men ran off in fear.

She said, "You say you love me,
Yet mock me with your lies.
Now tell me your great secret,
Dear Samson, strong and wise."

Day after day she teased him,
Until one day he said,
"At no time has a razor
Been used upon my head.

"It was my Lord's commandment
My hair and beard should grow,
And if I use a razor,
My strength will surely go."

One night as mighty Samson
Lay sleeping on the bed,
Delilah called a barber,
Who quickly shaved his head.

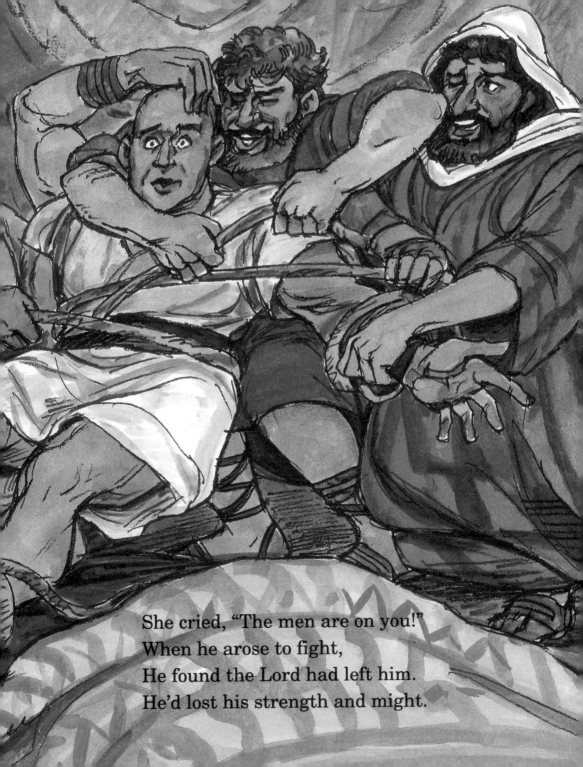

She cried, "The men are on you!"
When he arose to fight,
He found the Lord had left him.
He'd lost his strength and might.

They bound his hands behind him,
Put chains upon his feet.
They blinded him, then led him
Along the Gaza street.

Without God's power to help him,
Bald Samson, weak and blind,
Was shackled to the mill wheel,
The prison wheat to grind.

Day after day he labored,
But people did not know
That as the days were passing,
His hair began to grow.

One day when all were feasting,
Some said, "Bring Samson here.
He'll be our clown to cheer us,
No more a man to fear."

They led him to the temple
Between the pillars high.
He placed his hands upon them,
His face turned to the sky.

He prayed, "O Lord, forgive me
For sinful, selfish ways.
Avenge, dear God, my sightless eyes,
And let me end my days."

The God of Israel heard him
And gave him strength once more.
He pushed the temple pillars.
The roof crashed with a roar.

Three thousand who had gathered
To praise a god of stone,
Fell dead along with Samson.
His work for God was done.

Dear Parents:

At a time when the Philistines were oppressing Israel, God's angel told Manoah's wife that she would have a son. He would be a Nazirite, a specially dedicated servant of God to deliver His people from the Philistines.

Samson's strength came, not from within himself, but from God's Spirit. When, in a moment of weakness, he revealed that the secret of his strength lay in his uncut hair, his enemies were able to cut it off and capture him.

Samson turned to God and asked Him to use him once again to save His people. With his hair long again and his strength restored, Samson pulled down the heathen temple and killed 3,000 Philistines.

God had a special purpose in life for Samson, just as He has placed you and your child in a special place in life for the purpose of serving Him. Celebrate the fact that the Holy Spirit has led you to believe in Jesus as your Savior. Pray together that you will follow His guiding.

The Editor